SORRY
I SLEPT ON YOUR FACE

SORRY
I SLEPT ON Y♥UR FACE

Breakup Letters from Kitties
Who Like You but Don't Like-Like You

JEREMY GREENBERG

Andrews McMeel Publishing®

a division of Andrews McMeel Universal

Andrews McMeel Publishing
a division of Andrews McMeel Universal
1130 Walnut Street, Kansas City, Missouri 64106

www.andrewsmcmeel.com

www.jeremygreenberg.com

16 17 18 19 20 TEN 10 9 8 7 6 5 4 3 2 1

ISBN: 978-1-4494-7793-6

Library of Congress Control Number: 2016936007

Editor: Patty Rice
Art Director: Holly Ogden
Production Manager: Tamara Haus
Production Editor: Erika Kuster

ATTENTION: SCHOOLS AND BUSINESSES
Andrews McMeel books are available at quantity discounts with bulk purchase
for educational, business, or sales promotional use. For information,
please e-mail the Andrews McMeel Publishing Special Sales Department:
specialsales@amuniversal.com.

For Barbara, the love of my nine lives.

With eternal thanks to Casey Dean and the support of the entire San Diego Humane Society.

Dear Human with a Headache,

There comes a time in every kitty's life when he realizes coming out of the back bedroom during a party only leads to disappointment. I don't care how much fun I have zipping through everyone's legs and licking fallen French fries, sooner or later I find myself at the bottom of a punch bowl, apparently having killed a mouse. I don't like the kitty I become at these parties. I'm not saying you have to completely get rid of your humans. But it's time you start matching my level of commitment to this relationship. You never see me inviting my feral feline friends over to sit on our couch and drink milk until they sneak into the garage to mate. From now on, if you want to see your friends you can do it like I do—perched on a windowsill as they walk by the house.

Act broken and you'll get fixed,
Webster

I'm tired of partying with your friends
Kitty: Webster

You are under my power
Kitty: Mishka

Dearest Pet,

I, the one and only Mastermind Mishka, am not worried that you found my secret tinfoil ball bunker under the couch. I've got a second stash behind the bed! Your oversized boulder of a human brain could never anticipate such a strategy. I will keep "losing" tinfoil balls until I have all the tinfoil in the house. Then, you'll run to the store to buy more, never the wiser that I'm in the bathroom chewing on your toothbrush. You can't stop me!

But I do enjoy keeping you around, human. That's why I stay inside despite knowing that you leave the door open for approximately one minute every Wednesday to take out the trash. And when the postman rings the doorbell, the dog barks and distracts you from noticing that a cat of my diabolical talent could easily dart outside. Why leave when I know that you can never resist my gaze. You are powerless to my impenetrable tractor beam of evil kitty cuteness. Do you hear that ticking? That's not a bomb, it's the oven timer. I expect a piece of chicken with my dinner.

Obey!
Mishka

Dear It's Just Hay Fever,

I'm not judging you, and I'm sure there is a cat out there who would love to indulge your masochistic desire to erupt in a sneeze spaz every time you touch her fur. But have you thought about *why* you love to dress me up as a flower? How did this sick fantasy come about to make you wish I was both pollen *and* dander? I don't mean to upset you, and I can see just touching me brings tears to your eyes. But you have to ask yourself where this allergy kink is headed. Next you'll ask me to dress like a peanut and wear a latex glove on my tail. I love being your cat, but I'm not comfortable being your sadistic sneeze inducer.

Go wash your face,
Rose

You obviously have some sick allergy fetish
Kitty: Rose

I'm done looking the other way
Kitty: Simba

Dear Unperceptive Pesterer,

I can't sit back any longer and let you put this toy raccoon on my head. If I don't look adorably perturbed and run away, before you know it you'll be draping your sweaty gym socks across my body. You'll throw towels over me when I'm sleeping and laugh if I don't wake up. And I shudder to mention those times you've been so bold as to startle me out of a dead slumber with a face fart. You can't build a relationship just annoying me for your amusement. I'd never do that to you. Sure, I love to prevent you from folding your laundry. But you're so cute when shooing me away. You should see how funny your face looks when furiously refolding all your pants! And I enjoy attacking your feet when you walk by me early in the morning. But that's just my good-natured way of watching your face turn Garfield orange as you scream in pain. Ha! If I only had a camera.

But putting a raccoon on me—that's got to end.

See it from my side,
Simba

Dear Jet-setter,

Don't worry about me, I'll be fine here at your sister's house. Go on your vacation, I'll still be here when you get back. And by here I mean exactly right here in my cat carrier. I'm just a cat. Why do my feelings matter? Your sister's house is great. Seriously. Even though she has two dogs who hate me. It's good to live in terror for a week—it puts fur on the chest. So please, go do whatever it is that's more important than me. And don't bother unpacking my stuff, because this is a surprisingly spacious cat carrier. Hardly any of my fur sticks out the side holes, there's a great view of the carpet, and as of about ten minutes ago, there's an indoor bathroom in the back corner.

So have a great time. And when you get back, don't even bother trying to cuddle with me. I wouldn't want to disrupt your life with my love and companionship.

Conveniently yours,
Bailey

This relationship is going nowhere
Kitty: Bailey

Do whatever, man—I'm flexible
Kitty: Omar

Dear Control Freak,

Omar is no longer uneducated mail-order immigrant kitty. Omar lives in big house now, and knows how to be fancy house cat. That's why Omar only sleeps in the finest crystal. Omar doesn't sleep on floor like dog. Omar sleeps on table like human after New Year's Eve. Omar is comfortable. Omar make promise to himself on day of adoption never to let anyone stand in the way of where he dreams. Human yells at Omar to get butt off dishes. Maybe human sees how at peace is Omar and learns something. Omar no sleep with pillow under legs for lumbar support. Omar no take yoga class. Why Omar listen to uncomfortable human? Why Omar get off table? Maybe human get *on* table. Omar want to love human, but human must first love self. Omar love self, especially when self asleep on table.

Chillax,
Omar

Dear Pet Attention Deficit Disorder,

Why am I howl-yelling? Because I was ready to eat ten minutes ago while you were still asleep. How can you sleep when I'm so hungry? I'm howling because yesterday you came home ten minutes later than normal. Do you have any idea how worried I was (that no one would feed me)? I'm howling because I saw a cat on TV. Why do you allow other cats to come into my house through the TV? I'm howling because I smell a mouse in your walls. You think I scratch at them because I hate the color of paint you chose? I do, but that's not why I'm howling. I'm howling because you're still trying to sleep. Why are you trying to sleep while I'm trying to howl? You think my howling is hurting this relationship? If you would simply know what I'm thinking every moment of the day, this kitty wouldn't have to work so hard to catch your attention. I thought humans were the smartest species. Apparently you're not one for stereotypes.

Sheesh,
Miisa

If you'd just listen, I wouldn't have to howl
Kitty: Miisa

I'm a full-grown cat and I'll do what I want
Kitty: Pusseidon

Dear Reason I Love Liver Treats,

I know you wish I wasn't constantly seeking comfort in the bottom of a box. You'd prefer I brought my safety issues to you and snuggled. I admit that when I see a box, I'll climb in no matter how smashed I'll get. Before I know it I'm twisted and curled, wondering if I'll ever be able to straighten up again. You say it affects our relationship, and that you dread opening packages because it means I won't be emotionally available for hours. And I'm no box snob. I'll sit in big boxes, small boxes, I'll even sit in a dirty pizza box. So what if I come out a bit sauced? I bathe more than you do. I don't see the problem.

Look, you knew I was into boxes before we met. Do I say anything when you eat oranges? No, I completely ignore your revolting citrus habit. For this relationship thingy to work, I expect you to ignore me with the same respect I ignore you.

Your creature of habit,
Pusseidon

Dear Superstar Human Howler Katy Perry,

I promise you I'd never stalk a celebrity, unless she had untied shoelaces. But you'd probably find that cute, since you are a well-known cat lover! You are my favorite human! Which is why I'm asking if you'll be my human date to my shelter's adoption ball. A lot of celebrities now go to formal events with unknown cats, and I'd purr forever if you said yes. You can even bring your precious Kitty Purry, since I know she's been your cat for a very long time. I'm sure she wouldn't mind that I'm much younger and cuter. I'd never do anything to come between you and Kitty Purry. Though if you wanted to adopt me, I wouldn't be opposed. Did you know Taylor Swift has *two* kitties in her entourage? Olivia and Meredith. How do you feel about her kitty crew being bigger than yours?

Please write me back soon, Katy! If I don't hear from you, I'll ask Taylor Swift to be my date and you'll be dead to me.

Your biggest fan,
Pekoe

Behind every Katy Perry there's a Kitty Purry . . .
and I'd hate to see that change
Kitty: Pekoe

It's because you make me feel trashy
Kitty: Bitsy

Dear Unreceptive,

Do you have any idea what it does to a kitty's self-esteem to constantly be yelled at to stop humping stuffed animals, not to climb the Christmas tree, or quit letting the dog's tongue be your toilet paper? You start one three-alarm fire and suddenly you aren't allowed on the kitchen counter for fear you'll drop another toy mousy in the toaster. You think you're the only one who likes a hot breakfast? I try to show my love to you, and all you can say is, "Yuck, the cat's licking my head!" You don't get upset when the dog licks you, and we all know where that tongue has been. So don't wonder why you've found me in the trash. It's very clear any attempt to love you is just a complete waste.

Pitifully yours,
Bitsy

Dear Cheating Heart,

I've tried to keep an open kitty mind to your feline video fetish. We've been together for seventy kitty years. Our relationship has survived the time I got lost during a move, the great bath of 2005, and who can forget our trial separation, which you frequently dismiss as that time you had to fly back east for your mom's funeral. But how do you think I feel when you spend all day gawking at gingers and salivating over Siamese? You're going to make me regret all the years I've spent sleeping on your face. You act like I'm not exotic enough for you, but deep down you know you're a tabby chaser. You think any of your fantasy cats would accept a dry food diet? They'd never sleep on your face for fear of dirtying their butts on your oily forehead. But I love you enough to know that your face and my butt are a perfect match.

I'm willing to wait until you tire of those cell phone felines, but until then the only way you'll feel fur on your face is if you grow a beard.

With patience,
Lilly

If it's one thing cats love, it's photos of other cats
(and you're making me sorry I slept on your face)
Kitty: Lilly

When it comes to my heart, you've been benched
Kitty: Mufasa

Dear Clueless Can Tapper,

I don't need a human to care for my needs! I'm a strong, independent kitty who can't be tempted by your cutesy names or wet food promises. I don't need a cozy cat condo! I have found a perfectly suitable rotted bench under which I am completely camouflaged. You think I'm just some lap cat? You think a few strokes is all I need to feel complete? I'm descended from lions! I need to feel the wind on my fur, hear the scurry of beetles, and smell multiple sources of urine. You think I'm scared that it's about to rain? I've been in the bathroom when the showerhead pointed the wrong way.

I realize that I'm currently totally invisible to the human eye. But if you could see me, you'd see just how happy I am without you.

Please leave the garage open,
Mufasa

Dear Feline Fashionista,

Of course I love this handmade cat hat. I wouldn't risk our relationship with some backhanded catty opinion. You are clearly a cat-fashion visionary, and next year every kitty will howl at their human to dress them like a stoned snowboarder. The poof of yarn at the top is what really shows off your understanding of what cats want on their heads. That clump of waving strings is sure to aggravate any nearby felines, inviting a merciless flurry of paw swats. That's getting noticed! How did you know every cat wants to wear the equivalent of a kick-me sign? Let me also rave about how these earflaps make it impossible to hear even the loudest howls of a passing cat's laughter. A cat in this hat can rest assured that not only will other kitties swat him senseless, he won't even hear them coming.

But honestly, I love it.

Thanks so much,
Seiji Coo San

The meanie in the beanie
Kitty: Seiji Coo San

I'm not ready for more kids
Kitty: Whiskers

Dear Broken Biological Clock,

I'm not one of those cats who dismisses all children as crazy tail pullers. I do appreciate what they have to offer—mostly table scraps and abandoned glasses of milk. But you and the man human have been locking me out of the bedroom quite a bit lately, and I want to warn you that I'm not sure I can handle the responsibility of sticking my filthy paw in *two* cereal bowls every morning. I mean, have you thought about what it's going to be like on Sunday mornings when the new child wants to climb into bed and snuggle, but she can't because the cat's taking up half the bed and won't move? I just don't think it's fair to bring a child into that world.

Hmph,
Whiskers

Dear Blurred Boundaries,

You're obviously a bit new at this crazy cat lady thing, judging by the fact that it appears you're trying to brew tea from my butt fur. Let me offer some rules so you know the difference between being adorably eccentric, and expecting me to answer the phone when you're in the shower. And please don't be embarrassed or offended. Some of your confusion is my fault. I did stick my paw into your water glass when you weren't looking. I just didn't think you'd develop a taste for it. If you ever catch me drinking your water again, pour it out. I'm glad you're comfortable sharing. But never forget that my face can reach parts of my body that yours can't. And just because I lick the salt from your arms doesn't mean you should lick my head like you're my momma cat. Cat saliva is a natural antiseptic. Your saliva is a mixture of Diet Coke and Oreos. Every time you lick me, I have to lick myself again. It's enough to make me hide in your daughter's suitcase.

Just stop trying to impress me. You're already plenty crazy.

Slightly terrified,
Duncan

Would you like some tea? I'm serving Earl Grey Tabby
Kitty: Duncan

Are you toetally committed to this relationship?
Kitty: Kitty

Dear Fancy Feet,

How am I supposed to bite your toes as hard as I can if you're gonna be so sensitive? Even when I politely wait until you're sound asleep before trying to draw blood, you act like I'm some feral foot freak. All I want is a little bonding time and to kill your toes dead. A successful indoor kitty relationship requires honesty and a high pain threshold. If I knew you were weird about toe attacks, I'd have ignored you during adoption day and been cute for the woman with the pierced lip. She'd appreciate a good puncture wound.

Love hurts,
Kitty

Dear Old Maid,

First of all, let me thank you for feeding me the same thing every day for fifteen years. I sometimes think my tongue doesn't want to go back in my mouth for fear of having to endure yet another gag on the same powder-dry kibble. You think you're doing me a favor by feeding me this senior cat food crap. All it does is remind me I'm an old kitty who can't remember the last time he tasted tuna. And don't think I can't see how you look at me. It's not like *you've* gotten any younger. I might've developed a perma-wink, but you've got blue worms up and down your legs. We both know I'm not the only one who doesn't always make it to the box in time. The difference is I don't rudely stare at you wondering when you'll finally go to the big shoebox in the sky. No, I savor our time together and give thanks that I only have to look at you through one eye.

Turn on the heater,
Sher Khan

You ain't exactly Best in Show yourself
Kitty: Sher Khan

It's not you, it's me—and them
Kitty: Oliver

Dear Sweetie,

Sorry, I did get your calls. I know I didn't come running when you said my name all cutesy and high-pitched. I also heard you shaking my treats as you called my name again, followed by the desperate jingle of my toys. Thank you. You're so sweet, and it was tempting. All those things are wonderful, and you're wonderful. But right now I can't be the cat you want me to be. I do love (and am legally registered to) you. That's why I think we should take a break. I'm not saying we're over, although if you meet a cat who can sleep through your night terrors, restless legs, sleepwalking, and thunderous flatulence, I'll be happy for you. Luckily I've found a group of friends in your kid's room who understand that I just need to sleep without fear of being thwacked by one of your convulsing limbs. But we'll totally see each other. In fact, I'll come by the kitchen tomorrow and you can pet me while I eat.

XOXO,
Oliver

Dear Door Locker,

I'm not angry. I just want to know the truth. Whose shoes are these? And don't lie. They belong to that so-called "niece" of yours, don't they? The same niece who is supposedly so scared of cats that you had to move my food and litter into the frigid garage, forcing me to suffer through frozen-pawed poops. The same niece who, despite being so *terrified* of kitties, hasn't stopped pestering me since she kicked off these stinky shoes and set up her stuffed animals as squatters on the sunniest spots of *my* back bedroom. She's been here five minutes and already rubbed me the wrong way so much my fur looks punk. Then she tells me I'm a nice kitty, not a scary kitty, and tries to hug me! Insecure much? And why is she so scared of kitties? Is it because one once hissed at her? Did she ever consider that whichever cat hissed at her was simply tired of having half-eaten crackers balanced on his forehead?

I'll be under the couch until your sister returns to claim these stinky shoes and the homewrecker they came with. I'll eventually learn to forgive you, but it won't be easy and could take as long as thirty seconds.

Disregards,
Cino

Is your niece afraid of cats? Or the competition?
Kitty: Cino

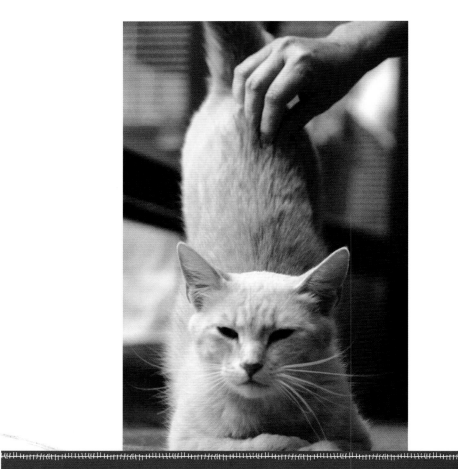

You know this is just a booty call
Kitty: Genifur

Dear Itch-Scratcher,

You never feed me on time. I'm always stuck outside when you leave for work. You haven't replaced the batteries in my laser pointer in two months, and mushrooms are sprouting in my litter box. You said you'd buy me a condo, but I sleep on a towel you stole from the gym. I don't have a feather toy. There's nothing worth looking at from your windowsills. Your kids are loud, your friends are louder, and your curtains are so heavy that not one streak of light can sneak in to brighten my days. But the one thing you do right, you do so right. Keep scratching.

Love,
Genifur

Dear Concoctor of Cat Runs,

One of the causes of tension in cat-human relationships is that humans don't think cats appreciate how hard they work to make us happy. I don't think that's true. For example, you just built me this cat run, for which you think I should be thrilled. And what cat wouldn't be thrilled spending a day so frustratingly close to an actual garden that his kitty mind is driven mad with the unsatisfied desire to bop a bug. I'm going to show my appreciation tonight after you've gone to bed by digging the dirt out of every houseplant. I will spend every ounce of my pent-up bug-bopping aggression covering your carpet in chewed philodendron leaves and potting soil. You obviously thought a contraption that walls off my instincts from the outside world with a sheet of chicken wire would be thoughtful. I appreciate your trying to make Rocco kitty happy, and when you wake up to find your carpet covered in my dirty paw prints, I will be.

Much appreciated,
ROCCO

Gee, thanks for almost letting me outside
Kitty: Rocco

My mother was right about you
Kitty: Petunia

Wow Human,

I remember when I was a kitten, my mommy cat said that humans would never let you bite them the way she let me bite her teat. Boy, was she right. That's not to mention how you shriek and curse at me when I innocently just want to smell your nipples. Geez. Do you suckle your mother with that mouth? What did you expect when you gave me a saucer of milk? Just like water, every cat prefers to drink from the faucet. You also get all bent out of shape when I want a whiff of your butt. Why is it gross for me to learn more about the human with whom I've chosen to spend the rest of my life? If you really wanted us to be close, your butt would be an open book. You're always welcome to visit my library.

When we met, you said you wanted to have a complete kitty-human relationship. Right now I give it just 3 out of 4 fangs.

In snarling sincerity,
Petunia

Dear Mrs. Claws,

Every year you get so wrapped up in this Christmas thing that you completely forget to give me your undivided attention. So in an effort to strengthen our bond, I've knocked over your candy basket to better acquaint myself with this tradition. I want to understand why on this holiday we knock candy canes and chocolates off the table instead of expensive, fragile vases and the permanently staining glasses of pomegranate juice that kitties knock off tables during the rest of the year. Is it because candy canes are long and skinny? Do they represent all the snakes and lizards good kitties get on Christmas? And why do we knock chocolates off the table? Chocolate is bad for kitties. Do naughty kitties get chocolate on Christmas? Of course, Pippin kitty has never been bad, so I'm sure the candy canes are mine. But I'll still knock the chocolates onto the floor for your other cats. They've been very naughty.

Confectionately yours,
Pippin

It's time to knock it off right now!
Kitty: Pippin

I'm just scared you'll grow bored with me
Kitten: Godzilla

Dear Soul Mate Candidate,

It's not that I want to remain feral my whole life. I've fantasized of fireplaces and refusing to let you make the bed. But right now we're both young and new to each other. What happens in a year, or two years, when your Facebook friends can't bear to see another photo of "that *wild* kitten you found"? You're attracted to me because I'm playing hard to take to the vet. But aren't you worried about what happens when the chase ends and I accept you as my forever mommy? Will I always come running to greet you at the garage door? What if I become one of those cats you find asleep in the same spot I was in when you left? Are you going to run out on me to start "volunteering" at the Humane Society?

What I'm saying is let's just take it slow. Things are good right now and I also still get free food from your neighbor.

Hugs,
Godzilla

Dear Royal Pain,

Not only did you forget to shut the door, you failed to warn me that the neighbor's dog thinks kitties taste like kibble. I escaped the confused canine's clutches with barely a scratch, and made it home only to be punished for *your* mistake. Like I'm the one with the highly evolved door-shutting hands. Apparently all those fancy human fingers are good for is pointing blame. You should be the one wearing this pink piece of crap Elizabethan collar! I don't need a cone of shame. My only shame is in being with a human who thinks a self-cleaning kitty needs a plastic plate around her neck. I'm sure it was fashionable in Queen Elizabeth's time to wear a cone of shame. She probably invented it during an embarrassing time in her life when she couldn't stop biting her butt. Humans of her day rarely bathed. Their backsides probably itched from bedbugs. Or maybe Queen Elizabeth accidentally let her pet loose, but unlike you, she was willing to take responsibility.

Either way, just do a better job shutting doors. I don't want to see you let the best thing in your life get away.

Just really disappointed (and a bit itchy),
Molly

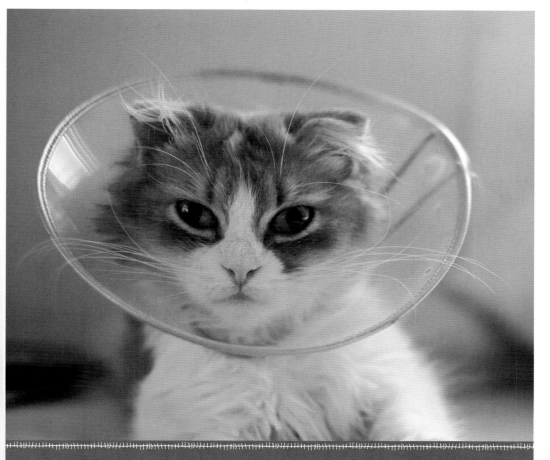

Is this your idea of treating me like a queen?
Kitty: Molly

**Please let me into your heart so I can immediately
ask to go back out**
Kitty: Lusia

Dearest Heat Source,

I know it must've come as a surprise that after all the scratching at this door to finally let me sleep in the bedroom every night, I've up and found somewhere new. Please don't be hurt. Sometimes a cat meets a new surface and then must sleep on that surface for a month straight for no reason. I never thought I'd be the kind of cat who liked throw rugs. But that new one didn't have a trace of funky cat dander. Unlike everything else in this house, it didn't have an ounce of my fur. I guess opposites do attract. At least at first. It must've just been a spring fling, because now that it's winter my relationship with the rug has gone cold. I'm not asking for you to forgive me. Just to open the door.

You know you can't say no,
Lusia

Dear Uncommitted,

I'm just concerned that you're not into me as much as I'm into you. When was the last time you watched *me* pee? I watch you every morning. And if you accidentally lock the door to the bathroom, don't I beat on it until you let me in? Don't I howl at you when my bowl's empty but you're in the shower? When you're hungry, I lick myself right in front of you on the kitchen table. I've never left you alone to eat. I follow you back and forth across the house all day, getting underfoot and tripping you as you run to your phone. I've been there for you at every step of this relationship. I sleep on your bed. Do you ever sleep on mine? I live in your house. Do you ever come over to my cat condo? You really need to think about what it means to put a collar on it. I expect to be treated with equality. I expect as much of the blanket as you do. Why can't you look me in the eyes and be honest when I'm hogging too much of the comforter? Instead it just feels like you start pulling away.

Codependently yours,
Whiskey

What are you thinking? Is it about us?
Kitty: Whiskey

Orders are orders, babe
Kitty: Kingston

Dear Forlorn Fiancé,

I'd love nothing more than to stay and cuddle, but I've been called up to the elite adorable kitty attack squadron. There's an enemy team of teething toys on the other side of the couch, and without me the rest of the litter could be biting off more than they can chew. That's why I'm not ready to settle down with you, even though I could use a nap. There will be a time for falling asleep under your shirt. I too dream of a future in which you're so depressed that you give me all-day belly rubs. Right now, I must keep the world safe from unfamiliar shadows and untied bathrobes. Don't wait for me. If I don't make it back, I fell asleep on the other side of the room.

Purr soon,
Kingston

Dear Security Blanket,

Stop your sweating and be thankful. You're not the only suitor on whom I could've sat. The dog is *always* looking at me and wagging his tail. And that dunce doesn't complain about allergies or get grossed out by whatever is stuck to the bottom of my tail. He understands that occasionally a kitty needs her space, which also includes any space on your body that happens to be warmer than my cold, fuzzy butt. Every time I need my space that just so happens to be on top of your airways, you try to cuddle me against your not-as-warm chest. Your desire to breathe has become a real control issue. Kitty relationships require trust, and I would never suffocate you. That would significantly decrease your body temperature.

Warm regards,
Pulgone

I just need my space (and most of yours)
Kitty: Pulgone

ACKNOWLEDGMENTS

First and foremost, I want to thank my A+ agent, David Fugate, for being really, really good, and my excellent editor, Patty Rice, for teaching me the intricacies of timing. To Kathy Hilliard, Holly Ogden, Kirsty Melville, and everyone at Andrews McMeel for their loving care in cultivating all our books. Thank you to Andrew Norelli for his saintly patience, Jess Smith and Sam Thorpe for believing, Lauren and Jon for ignoring me when required, Arnie and Adele for being perfect, Jose Tapia for the art of eight limbs, Lane Foster always, Ben and Seth for being my reason, and all my fellow cat lovers who allow me to share the gift of happiness that's never farther than a fuzzy little face. Thank you!

PHOTOGRAPHER CREDITS

Laura Andrade, Petunia, page 48, and Rose, page 11; Sonbol Ansari, Bailey Bear, page 15, Mishka, page 8, and Pippin, page 51; Stefano Burrini, Cino, page 43; Nancy Canty, Sher Khan, page 39; Samantha Carlton, Pusseidon, page 20, and Genifur, page 44; Bonancini Emanuela, Pulgone, page 63; Daniel Glenn, Omar, page 16; Yasemin Göl and Mert Baltacıoğlu, Godzilla, page 52; Frank Gronendahl, Lili, page 27; William Haas, Kingston, page 60, and Webster, page 7; Akimasa Harada, Molly, page 55; Natalia Kraemer, Whiskey, page 59; Joan De Lurio, Seiji Coo San, page 31; Umberto Mannarino, Mufasa, page 28; Maple Images, Oliver, page 40; Samantha Melton, Whiskers and Kennedy Grace, page 32, and Kitty, page 36; Adrian Midgley, Pekoe (Empress of the Universe), page 23; Antti Mikkonen, Miisa, page 19; Ariskina Oksana, Lusia, page 56; Jodi Payne, Simba, page 12; Dawn Marie Rappa, Duncan, page 35; Ashton Sookie Photography, Rocco, page 47; Jeffreyw, Bitsy, page 24.